Anita Frost

DREAM THE IMPOSSIBLE DREAMS

DISCOVER ENTREPRENEURSHIP SET UP FOR SUCCESS

For Information Address:
Anita Frost
Services
Rebekah Billingham
Editor
83 Ducie Street
Manchester
M1 2JQ

CONTENTS

"Twenty years from now you will be more disappointed by the things that you didn't do than by the ones you did do. So throw off the bowlines. Sail away from the safe harbor. Catch the trade winds in your sails. Explore. Dream. Discover."

Mark Twain

"Great people do things before they're ready. They do things before they know they can do it. Doing what you're afraid of, getting out of your comfort zone, taking risks like that- is what life is. You might be really good. You might find out something about yourself that's really special and if you're not good, who cares? You tried something. Now you know something about yourself."

Entrepreneur, Amy Poehler

Dear Rebekah,

Thank you for being in my life.

all my love

INTRODUCTION

Research has shown that thousands of men and women across different ages, at some point have, toyed with these ideas: "I wonder what it would be like to have my own business" or "I would love to have my own business". For some, this thought is as far as their story goes. The rest bravely confront fears to start a new adventure.

Research into successful business owners has shown that they each shared something very similar in the way they positioned and equipped themselves in the earlier stages of getting started. Over their business timeline, this positioning led them to seeing that it is possible to set your own sail and flow in the direction of your dreams.

Success achieved from taking ideas, plans and a vision and breaking them down into small step-by-step actions.

Taking these actions has moved many towards reaching goals, learning the art of working smart and stepping over obstacles as they occur. Focusing on what's required to moving forward sets many on course to making dreams possible. Starting a business or planting your idea, it's vitally important to surround your ideas with the best ingredients for growth.

Entrepreneurs grow and evolve from the inside out, collecting knowledge and skills whilst adapting to changes as the journey progresses. Entrepreneurship built by one individual can change the course of an economy and create opportunities for generations who follow. As you move through the pages of this book, you will find stories and pointers to guide you through your own journey as an entrepreneur.

Inside knowledge has been laid out to inspire, prepare and propel your business. Each chapter gives you the opportunity to enhance your knowledge through self reflection exercises to raise your awareness of what you set out to achieve. Are you ready to get started? It's time to brush off any old, unhelpful habits that could be keeping you from unlocking your true potential.

CHAPTER ONE

MANAGING & DEVELOPING YOU

What is an entrepreneur?

An entrepreneur sees an opportunity that others do not fully recognise. They have a thirst to implement their strategy in order to improve the performance of an existing or new industry. They are resilient and persistent in their self-belief as they prepare for and realise opportunity through smart work and commitment, adapting to undertake the learning necessary to becoming a leader who will have a strong and lasting impact. Entrepreneurs, as well as being prepared to work out of their comfort zone, understand that their achievements are the result of lots of small steps compounding over time. They are prepared to utilise their unique blend of talents and abilities to support the manifestation of their vision into reality.

When growing into entrepreneurship, it can be easy to become diverted or discouraged by negative or unconstructive criticism from those who lack the ability and knowledge to support you on your quest to make a profitable future for yourself. However, there is a way to side-step these distractions: take on as much positive advice as you can. You can allow positive encouragement to be a resource that you pass on and invest into others. Keeping your business and your future unpolluted opens the door to more opportunities, causing you and your idea to thrive and grow into the successful business you set your sights on.

Start by getting to know yourself and focusing on what is important to you in order to set a strong foundation of clarity and purpose from which to build your dream. At the outset, begin by defining the reason WHY you are doing what you are doing. This will help create and maintain a clearly oriented mind-set.

REFLECTION EXERCISE ONE:

Ask yourself the following questions:

1. Why have you chosen to start your own business?
2. What do you already know?
3. What do you still need to learn?
4. Write down the pros and cons of starting up a business.

TIP

A positive and focused mind at the beginning can lead to a successful business in the long run

Highlight your priorities in order of importance. Then you can identify where your energy should be focused at the beginning of your endeavour. It helps to have both a short term and a long term reason for getting started. Break these down into bite sized chunks to define where you see your

Anita Frost

idea/business going, and when you would like your milestones to take place.

Reflection Exercise Two:

Write down your goals for these different time frames

1. Next week:

2. Next month:

3. Next three months:

4. Next year:

5. Next five years:

The more you familiarise yourself with your reason for starting, and the more you commit to putting your belief into action and actively moving in the direction you want to go in, the quicker you will be able to pick yourself up when the challenging days come your way - and they will, as entrepreneurs are only human beings after all!

Just like a newborn baby, entrepreneurship does not come with an instruction manual. Assign yourself compartments of time in which to put your ideas and thoughts into action to move you onwards. It is best to have a steady approach, and spread out what needs to be accomplished over a substantial amount of time. When you exercise patience and are prepared to take small steps one at a time, you will be less likely to encounter the disappointment of crashing and burning out. Crashing and burning out happens when you try to move faster than you are realistically able to,

Give yourself credit where credit is due. CELEBRATE the steps you make, no matter how small they may seem. See your business as a bank account, and positive thoughts and actions as deposits that you put into your account that cause it to grow, adding to what you already have. Negative thoughts and the resulting actions can begin to gradually take away from what you have gained because they bring feelings of defeat that can lead to failure if left unchecked, withdrawing and decreasing what you have in your account. Too many withdrawals will put your personal investments of time and effort out of balance. Take charge of your business and stay committed to learning and working to overcome obstacles.

It is important to recognise your negative emotions as quickly as you can, because they can send you off track and prevent you moving forward. Becoming aware of what triggers you to think negatively will help you to keep things in perspective, and ultimately stay focused on tasks in hand such as maintaining your priority list. In business, uncontrolled emotions like frustration, doubt, and worry can lead to delay, potentially pushing the manifestation of your dream further away from you. It is good to think ahead and plan what positive action you will take if you find yourself struggling with these feelings further down the line.

Reflection Exercise Three:

Complete the following statements to support your preparation:

1. When I feel tired - I am going to:

2. When I feel like I am hitting a wall - I am going to:

3. To lift my positivity – I enjoy to:

4. When someone shares a bad opinion of me or my business – I am going to:

There will be times when your actions have results that are not like what you hoped they would be. In unsettling moments like this, it helps to change your perspective on any unwanted results by seeing it as a learning opportunity.

This way, the outcome will always be that you come out the other end having learned something new about yourself and, at the very least, you will know not to make that particular mistake again. Even seemingly negative circumstances can have good outcomes that you may not realise at first.

So, always keep an open mind...

Reflection Exercise Four:

Take a moment to list your skills and then think about how they can support you with your business planning:

Think of a time or situation, which produced unwanted results for you:

How did you feel at the time?

What did you learn?

Write three ways this learning process could support you within entrepreneurship:

1.

2.

3.

Reflection before problem solving is a highly effective process. A good way to do this is to write in pencil any unplanned or unwanted outcomes. Then underneath, on a new line (in pen) turn the statement around into a positive one.

Here Is An Example:

Unwanted Outcome

We don't speak as much now I started my business (Pencil)

Outcome Turned Around

I am grateful for those who encourage me in setting up my business (Pen)

Once finished, simply rub out the negative statement you wrote in pencil. This is a great exercise that can be applied to both personal and business development. Mastering the art of developing yourself allows you to see outcomes without to many hindering emotions, putting you in a good position to start making the changes needed to move you and your business in the right direction.

TIP

*Have patience, work smart, show up for
success. Be 100% present in each task!*

Welcome each day as it comes, and every morning, make a note of four things that need to be actioned in order to take the small steps needed to make progress that day. Challenge yourself to complete the task you're least confident with, or don't really want to do FIRST! Do this each day without procrastinating or putting it to the bottom of your list for later. Each step you act on and learn from will gradually increase your productivity. Whatever happens, embrace the excitement of uncertainty. This is be a big part of being an entrepreneur, especially when just starting out.

Taking Your Ideas Forward

A man had an idea for a new voice-activated house alarm, but there was one problem: he had no money and no customers. What he did next was typical of an outstanding entrepreneur. After a lot of rational thinking, he convinced a DIY store to sell him the parts he needed to build them using the order he had just gained as proof he would be able to pay them back. He had help, of course. Two of his best friends who were unsure of his idea at first were soon on board when they realised that he was willing to take a risk. After a lot of work, late nights and a few disagreements, they eventually delivered the products on time and made a tidy profit on each device.

This story shows the importance of really believing in your idea in order to get others on board. You need evidence to override your senses and actions in every way to show investors and potential clientele that your product is worth investing in.

This is a clever way of having your business, products and services promoted. It backs up what we read earlier that starting a new venture is not done in a hop, skip and jump. You are setting up in the real world, where there are opposition and hurdles to get past.

Your lifestyle may become unbalanced as you build your business around other commitments, and might sometimes feel like a chaotic mess. This is where the butterfly effect comes in...

What is the butterfly effect? How is it relevant to being an entrepreneur? The scientific theory of the butterfly effect is that a single occurrence, no matter how small, can determine the course of the future. This could be true of you and your idea. Even if you have not taken flight yet, your idea can still be tweaked and modified, just like what happens to the caterpillar in its cocoon. This can be done by deepening your research according to what your product and services are geared towards.

Reflection Exercise Five:

Write your feelings down and then make a list of things that still worry you in pencil under the fear heading, and things that you have become fearless to under the fearless heading, as shown below:

Fear	Fearless

Once completed, take a moment to rewrite any fears as a fearless statement, e.g FEAR: "What if no one will buy from me?" FEARLESS: "Everyone is looking to pay for my service"

Your business may be just a thought at the moment, or it may already be up and running. No matter what stage you are at, your business still needs to grow and put down strong roots. Allow changes to take place where they are needed, so that you will be equipped for the next stages.

Do what you are born to do. When there are those moments when you think 'Wow, I'm not really sure I can do this,' and you push through them, that's when you will have breakthrough.

- Marissa Mayer

CHAPTER TWO

THE ART OF EFFECTIVE
COMMUNICATION & LEADERSHIP

*"Before anything else,
preparation is the key to success"*

- Alexandra Graham Bell

Effective communication is ESSENTIAL to all areas of our everyday life. Become at ease with yourself, and be aware of your tone of voice and body language, as well as reviewing other people's contributing thoughts whilst sharing the vision and the facts of your business.

Effective communication is a discussion between equals in which you are able to listen, hear, understand and respond to the other person without interrupting, and without the need to be right. Taking in another person's views or thoughts when it comes to similar problems or interests is vital to communicating with precision.

Projecting your voice tone can often determine how what you're saying is delivered to your listener. Things that can interfere with the sharing of your message include coughs, murmurs, groans and sighs. They have a big part to play when getting your ideas or visions across, as they could make you sound vague, and not as committed as you really are. Here is an example of a detailed and precise description of an enjoyable holiday: "The beautiful sun setting before me brings a gleaming light to the beautiful sand surrounding me. The sea is glittering and my body is warm with golden rays from a day at the beach. My face is touching the flow of the soft coast breeze. Sunset colours, shades of red, orange and yellow, shining brightly across the beach was such a beautiful picture".

On the flip-side, this is what a vague, non-committal description looks like: "Wellll...you know when I was on holiday...errrrmmm... well I had a great day at the beach and stayed to watch the sun set..... errrmmm.... it was nice."

With these examples in mind, take a moment think about what type of communicator you are.

Reflection Exercise One:

Jot down how you think you communicate best, reflecting on some past situations you have been in:

1.

2.

3.

If you are not clearly getting the point across regarding practicalities of the what, where, when and how of your business idea and plans, it is likely that this could lead to your listeners becoming confused, which can start off a chain reaction of misunderstandings and frustration, which could easily have been avoided if you had communicated clearly and coherently. You can take control by being a step ahead. Ask yourself, "who do I need to communicate with?" and "How do they communicate best?" The more you take the plunge and say what you are thinking, your confidence in how you phrase your thoughts will increase. This will lead to fewer hiccups along the way. Travelling in an unfamiliar place that is not signposted clearly, you feel confused and lost, unable to get your bearings. Likewise, being vague in your explanations may cause your listeners to experience something similar.

Walt Disney had a long way to go before the doors to his Disneyland theme park could be opened. The vision he had in his mind was so clear, yet when he communicated this to family and potential investors, they just couldn't see it the same way he did. What do you do when people cannot see your vision? Walt Disney began to put his vision into action because for some, seeing is believing.

He created more than eighty-one feature films and hundreds of short films. He earned more than 950 honours, including forty-eight Academy Awards. Success born from difficult challenges turned into important lessons with events that would, unknown to Disney at the time, create success later on.

At the age of twenty-two, he became bankrupt after the failure of a cartoon series in Kansas City. Believing there were people who could animate far better than him, he moved to LA to pursue a career as an actor. While in LA, Walt and his brother Roy realised there were no animation businesses in California, so they decided to fill this gap by pioneering one of their own, which led to them becoming the most successful team of brothers in Hollywood.

After World War Two, the company had over four million dollars of debt. Unable to pick up the pieces in America straight away, Walt Disney's company began producing their films overseas. To relieve stress he took up a new hobby; collecting miniature trains. This, as well as calming his nerves, began to unlock more ideas. Soon, he had a dream to create an amusement park with a train running around the outskirts.

He was determined to pursue this. He had to become solution focused. To raise the required start-up funds, he used his other talent and made a commitment to television. This decision was not initially approved by major Hollywood producers and, on several occasions, they informed him that they thought television production would ruin the movie business. Walt went with his gut instincts and courage, eventually gaining the finance needed to create Disneyland. This is an incredible example of what can be possible if you keep pushing through opposition.

Leadership

"Leadership is lifting a person's vision to high sights, the raising of a person's performance to a higher standard, the building of a personality beyond its normal limitations"

- Peter Drucke

Some of the greatest leaders who have gone before us appear to have something in common: the fight to win, and the willpower to achieve! Leaders keep the essence of their idea before them as they take action. They know very well what results they want from the energy and resources they have invested into their businesses, and, as such, are able to inspire the people in their teams to work with them to bring their idea to pass.

A leader is a person who guides from the front, carrying out what is required to produce great results. A leader's influence can unlock people's inner potential, encouraging them to become independent and develop new skills.

Manager or Leader

There may have been a time when you were managed in a workplace or even have been the manager. A manager is the person responsible for planning and directing the work of a group of individuals, monitoring their work, and taking corrective action to direct progress for a company. As you begin to lead your vision forward, note the differences within the these two roles.

Manager:	**Leader:**
Administers	*Innovates*
Maintains	*Develops*
Focuses on systems	*Focuses on people*
Follows structure	*Resolves issues without emotions*
Controls systems and people	*Inspires people*
Accepts the ways things are	*Challenges the way things are*
Has a short range view	*Has a long range perspective*
Manages tasks	*Creates leaders*

A leader can turn problems into opportunities, and will happily break the rules in order to get things done, while managers tend to be more focused on the ins and outs of the company and will try to minimise risks!

"Before you are a leader, success is all about growing yourself. When you become a leader, success is all about growing others".

- Jack Welch

Leaders are strong and effective in emphasising the importance of essential elements such as discipline, accountability and strategic planning in alignment with their own values, this empowers teams to grow. As a leader, your highest priority is to work on yourself, taking small and consistent steps to grow. The actions you take set a positive example to others around you. If you work smartly on yourself, you are likely to encourage others to do the same.

Taking The Lead:

During their early years, children are showered with praise and encouragement and given guidance in their early learning and growth. From trying new foods to taking our first steps, each of us are born into the world with an inner guidance system, which allows us to discover what feels good and not so good. Yet as we grow up, we lose touch with our inner guide, and we find ourselves absorbing the opinions, rules and conditions set by others, which, over time, drowns out and takes over our own guidance system. Leaders re-awaken and utilise their inner guidance system, learning quickly what they don't want, and then launching themselves into the direction of what they DO want, acknowledging each want as they become aware of it.

Reflection Exercise Two:

Answer the following questions about your own leadership role.

1. What type of leader are you?
2. What qualities do you already have?
3. Do you have the skills and integrity to lead others?

Reflection Exercise Three:

Think about your own leadership.

1. How can you develop your leadership within the following areas?

   a.) Ability:

   b.) Skill:

   c.) Behaviour:

2. Have you always been the kind of leader you are today, or have your character traits changed over time?

   a.) How?

3. Are you a stronger leader today than you were five years ago?

   a.) Why?

"Effective leadership is not about making speeches or being liked; leadership is defined by results not attributes"

Peter Drucker

This Peter Drucker quote defines great leadership in action. The leader strives to get results no matter what obstacles come their way, finding a way to move past obstacles and then teach their followers how to do the same. Leaders succeed because they are able to deal with the issues that need most to be eliminated. They create an excellent workforce and have a growing ability to become unaffected by the negativity of others.

As a leader, you never settle. There will always be ways to improve and expand on your skills. Even the greatest leaders throughout the world are still actively learning, from their own experiences and seeking the advice of others leaders, to discover the best possible ways to inspire and motivate their teams. Successful leaders know exactly what they want. Learning is a continuous practice throughout their movements within business. Ensure to never stop looking for opportunities to grow, expand and collaborate within your company, passing on the lessons you learn to those who also seek to grow within your teams.

Part of effective leadership is having a positive attitude towards others and the know how to build strong and enduring relationships with their clients, employees and new contacts. They choose to get involved by partnering with their employees and earning their respect, their trust, and their loyalty.

They don't do this, however, by keeping their opinions or thoughts to themselves. They really connect to people; involving them, engaging them, and letting them know that they are valued and respected members of the team. This mostly happens through the medium of word choices and conversations. The tone of a leader's conversation with their team is very powerful, as it plays a significant part in influencing people's motivation levels. If a leader communicates positively with their team and makes them feel encouraged and that their work is valued, they will be more likely to be productive and do their work to a higher standard.

Here are a few loose guidelines.

Firstly, asking your team questions such as "what do you think?" and "what can I do to help?" is a way to make them feel like their thoughts matter. Questions give people an open door to speak their minds and make an active contribution. Even simple things like saying please and thank you can make all the difference. In your own way, you can be supportive and let them know that you are there to help them. Messages such as 'I have time for you', "I've got your back" and "I know you can do this" can be given verbally, as well as being implied non-verbally, by your actions and overall attitude. All of these things add up, and can set the tone for a positive atmosphere in which the team can thrive and be excellent.

"The same wind and rain blows on us all. It is the set of the sails, not the direction of the wind that determines which way we will go."

- Jim Rohn

You may have uncertainties about the decisions that you make, you can be brave by continuing with your efforts despite trying to talk yourself out of it. Sometimes you do need to go down the road that has a lot of cracks and bumps in order to gain the results that you want. Being bold in the face of doubts will enhance your future prospects as a leader, and this can help your team to have the courage and willingness to carry on striving to reach their goals when the challenges come.

CHAPTER THREE

Increasing Positive Thinking & Actions

Going into the world of entrepreneurship can be a funny process, especially if you have been an employee or have been raised in non-entrepreneurial environment, because you will spend the early part of your journey unlearning everything you have learned so far.

Throughout our childhoods, we were learning and gathering pieces of information about life and the world around us, which contributed significantly to the way we think about and perceive life as adults. The information gathered was collected from parents, teachers, friends and other contributors who have influenced us to this point.

Our minds have stored up conversations, images, actions and new knowledge.

This collection is retrieved from our memory, and elements are played back into our day to day life and used in conversations, decisions making, and how we respond to the people around us. How we process each of these events with our thinking will play a significant part in determining our immediate futures.

From nursery through to high school and beyond, we have been shaped by our experiences, and the people that were a part of them. During each of these seasons, our time is spent with family members, friends and teachers, each one playing a part in contributing to our development and influencing us. We learn and copy the different ways they deliver their thoughts, approaches or agendas from a very young age, making us, in many ways, a product of our environments.

All this influence we received builds up our own individual way of thinking, and can eventually determine our future. Influence can condition or stretch our thinking, as we can often find ourselves implementing or acting out some of this influence into our own surroundings.

Reflection Exercise One:

List some people you have been influenced by over the last few years.

1. How have they influenced you?
2. Has their influence been positive or negative?
3. How does this show up in the way you think and conduct your life?

Tuning In

In a way, our thoughts are similar to the channels on a radio that we tune in and listen to. Each channel has a different set of sounds and messages that gets sent into the atmosphere. A radio offers many stations for us to tune into, because we don't all want to listen to the same thing. When starting a business, not everyone will be tuned into the same radio station as you, it is important to find the thought channel to suit your business and the direction in which you want it to go. It is obvious that every entrepreneur overall aim is for their business to go in a positive, constructive direction, allowing your thoughts to be tuned in to a negative channel, can results in your momentum becoming hindered. Tune into a positive thought channel, which reflects what you are wanting for the future of your business.

Which channel are you tuned into the most? Positive FM or Negative FM?

At some point we tune into both of these channels during our lifetime. The channel people tune into most frequently over their lifetime is a big contributing factor to their mindset, which can, in turn, influence their actions and the outcomes of these actions. When you hear your favourite song, your natural instinct is probably to turn it up and began to dance like nobody's watching. You enjoy the song, feeling the words and the rhythm. Maybe you even rewind the song back and play it again. Why? Because it feels good to you.

How many of us fill our days with the things that feel good to us? Probably not as much as we would like, as increasing responsibilities cause us to see enjoyment as a lower priority, so we slowly start to shut ourselves off from things that make us feel good. Actively seeking positive feelings can work towards higher success rates, as these feelings are not dependent on the opinions of others, or on what has gone right or wrong on any given day.

Yet so many people get stuck on Negative FM. This channel is limiting, as it shuts us off from opportunities to improve our quality of living, and keeps us trapped in bad habits so that we don't see change as an option. The polar opposite of Positive FM, this way of thinking is not compatible with possibility and forward momentum. Frequency projects a signal, and a signal attracts connections. The channel you are tuned into can, to an extent, determine your surroundings and the kinds of people you connect with.

Reflection Exercise Two:

What and who do you want to attract:

1. Into your business?

2. Why?

3. Into your family?

4. Why?

5. Into your friendships?

6. Why?

> "A positive attitude causes a chain reaction of positive thoughts, events and outcomes. It is a catalyst and it sparks extraordinary results."
> **- Wade Boggs**

A chain reaction is a sequence not only used in science. It can also be applied to relationships and businesses. There is a saying that goes "what you think about you bring about". This illustrates the fact that our thinking can start off a chain reaction in our lives. To reinforce a positive thinking pattern we should remind ourselves of what we have in our lives that we appreciate.

Every morning, shift your focus to what you appreciate by making a list of the things or people you are grateful for. Highlight your likes, your joys, and things that make you feel REALLY good. (Also try verbally expressing your appreciation out loud) Why do we wait to receive things before we become positive and thankful? What if we were thankful and appreciative towards all things around us, even before we have received them?

"What we think determines what happens to us, so if we want to change our lives we need to stretch our minds"

Dr Wayne Dyers

A negative mindset can impose great limitations upon your ability and willingness to stretch yourself to the capacity to reach for your dream. We cannot control how others think and play out their lives. We must focus on our own thoughts, as they are the frequency that determines how events and outcomes come into our reality. A positive attitude is an important first step towards initiating a virtuous cycle of progress, to support your business getting into a good momentum. If you think positively, you behave positively. Your frequency is then set to Positive FM, attracting an increase of good results.

As you progress into your venture, you will have many great opportunities to meet new people. Some of these introductions can open new doors for your venture, or some may hold you back. When any information or people present themselves to you, think carefully and weigh up the pros and cons of any offers.

Reflection Exercise Three:

Every time you meet somebody new in business, it is worth asking yourself the following questions and trying to answer them as honestly as you can.

1. Was this a good conversation?

2. Why was it good?

3. Was it bad? If so how can I turn this experience into a positive one?

4. What did I learn from this?

5. Do I need to ask some other questions or find out more to support my thinking?

It can become challenging to keep up a consistently positive attitude when things do not go to plan, and it seems like we have hit a wall. However, it is possible to turn these moments around by finding ways to turn the unwanted outcomes over for the best. Creating good habits can equip us to strengthen our Positive FM signal. For example, carrying out positive actions such as spontaneous acts of kindness is a great way to raise your frequency...This is just one way to work towards creating good habits, and prevent low moods and worry from limiting your mind.

Reflection Exercise Four:

The following exercise will show you how to get going. We have filled in the first two questions in to get you started.

Increasing Positive Actions

1. Smile. Why?
'a smile can travel along way cheering me up and others around me'

2. Say "thank you" more. Why?
'Because it raises my feelings of appreciation and makes the receiver feel valued'.

3. Get at least 15 minutes of sunshine every day. Why?

4. Surround yourself with positive people as much as you can. Why?

5. Disconnect from technology and connect to the natural. Why?

6. Read things that inspire you. Why?

7. Stay active every day. Why?

8. Do something that you truly enjoy every day. Why?

9. Compliment yourself regularly. Why?

10. Laugh often. Why?

The journey of raising your positive awareness will always be unfolding. Each time you get onto a positive frequency, a ripple effect is created into your surroundings. This is your key to taking hold of the ugly and turning it into something beautiful.

The Art of Allowing

Letting go, delegating or allowing someone else to hold the reins can be a challenge for many new leaders. The key to learning the art of allowing is to let be what needs to be. A wonderful example of this is the caterpillar's sensational journey towards allowing the release of its full potential.

The process of transformation for both caterpillars and entrepreneurs is challenging yet beautiful. The caterpillar starts as a dot attached to a leaf. How incredible it is to think that this dot evolves by using its natural instincts. The caterpillar is appreciative and resourceful as it quickly adapts to its surroundings. Days pass, and the tiny caterpillar inches its way up trees, discovering new heights. Its instincts draw it to know it has a purpose. An instinct increases their awareness to what's coming next as they move into position to allow them to become who they are meant to be. They begin to wait with no resistance, and their cocoon starts to form. Construction is under way as they prepare physically and mentally to take flight. The cocoon has served its purpose, and it is now time to embrace the new beginning.

This illustrates the art of allowing. Not once does the caterpillar complain, resist, make excuses or refuse to participate in what needs to be done...we encourage you as an entrepreneur to position yourself correctly: plan, adapt, learn, and speak positively even when signals from Negative FM come your way. Allow what is happening to happen, and celebrate the growing process.

CHAPTER FOUR

HOLDING & GROWING YOUR FINANCES

When someone is in debt, all their income is accounted for as soon as it arrives into the bank, leaving nothing or very little left over at the end of each month, meaning that year on year, they are barely getting by. For some, getting into debt can happen very quickly. For others, it can be a slow and gradual process where they feel like debt sneaked up on them out of nowhere later on in life. Many would love to know how to be released from debt, and to turn their situation around for the better.

Is it possible to live financially free? We have a choice at this point to either judge and be jealous or resentful towards individuals who are surrounded by wealth and prosperity or see the possibility to embrace this as a new opportunity for our own future. By digging a little bit deeper, you can financially educate yourself and take control of your own future.

Knowing The Difference:

Short Term Wealth: Can occur from one off circumstances, we have provided some examples.

- Work Bonus
- Compensation
- Inheritance
- Promotion
- Tax Returns
- Gifts

When short-term wealth is placed in to the hands of those who have minimal or no financial educated, the money they receive runs out within a very short period of time. These individuals are left wishing and longing for another short term wealth opportunity or moment to come back around again soon.

Long Term Wealth: Many individuals have accumulated a flow of long term wealth to surround them, each year adding to their financial cushions to elevate them towards a preferred way of living. Their first move is to begin working on themselves to become more financially aware and educated. Second step make a plan, how can they make a difference for others and thirdly select their preferred investment routes to line them up for living a life of financial freedom. Over time these repeated and committed behaviours can give anyone the opportunity to master and create ways to build upon long term financial security.

"To become successful, you need to invest in yourself, educating yourself in every aspect of life so that you are able to acquire the quality skill set. Identify your talents and find a way to turn them into an income generating vehicle"
- Anon

Reflection Exercise One

Where Am I Going?

1. What does financial freedom mean to you?

2. Do you want to create your own financial freedom?

3. Why?

4. Who has financially educated you so far?

5. Are they living financially free?

6. If so, what investment or plan did they use?

7. What investment or plan are you going to start with?

8. Why?

The Flash Family:

Meet the Flash family and their youngest son Joe. They are a family who show us an example; of the choices they had taken to hold and grow their family finances. As you read on ask yourself these questions, are you working for money? or is money working for you?

Joe grew up in a middle class family. His dad, a high income earner, worked long hours as an accountant. Joe's dad assured Joe's mum she would not need to work and could enjoy life at home raising the children. Anything either she or the children needed, he would always take care of. Joe enjoyed his childhood. He had great memories of having his mum and three siblings around, all getting on well together. Often they were treated with new gifts outside of their birthdays or Christmas, and travelled on two or three holidays each year as a family.

Both his parents supported and encouraged him and his siblings to work hard on their education and school achievements. His parents were strong believers that education was the foundation to set their children up for success in the future, just as Joe's father and grandfather had done.

Aged twenty, Joe was off to university with his sights set on becoming a doctor. With student finance secured and both his parents agreed in contributing to his cost of living, Joe's future was looking bright.

Joe spent the next five years at university. Once he had completed his degree, he added on a further two years of study to enhance his knowledge in practice to be a GP. As Joe was coming to the end of his last year in uni, it was time for him to gain some work experience in a practice. The university found a placement for Joe in a local practice not too far from where his parents lived.

Joe enjoyed his placement and made a very good impression. So much so, that towards the end of his work experience the team offered him a part-time position, depending on whether he achieved his estimated grades. This was the best news for Joe, and both his parents were completely over the moon and very proud of his achievements. With graduation day just round the corner, Joe was feeling very good about the direction his life was going.

"Many people take no notice of their money till they come to nearly the end of it. And others do just the same with their time"

- Wolfgang Van Goethe

Ten Years On

His part time role expanded into a full time doctor's role working around fifty hours per week. Joe now lived in a beautiful home with his wife and two daughters aged six and three. When not at work, Joe enjoyed his time with family going on days out and holidays. Some of his time was spent with friends playing golf. Joe wanted the same lifestyle for his wife as his mum had staying at home raising the children. Joe's wife was also happy to take on this family role.

The years passed quickly as they repeated the same activities. Their children grew fast. While Joe was at work one day, he received a call from his wife saying he would need to make his way over to the hospital as his father had become unwell. Over the last five years, Joe's dad had struggled with his health and had suffered a mini stroke over the last year.

Handing the rest of his appointments over to his team at the surgery, Joe made his way to the hospital to see his dad. Once he arrived at the hospital, he was greeted by both his mum and brother, who told Joe that his dad was very unwell and had suffered a major heart attack while returning back from work. The doctor had said his dad would need to stay in the hospital to recover and rest over the next few days.

This was very upsetting time for the family, unfortunately the news had not come to them as a great shock, Joe's dad was due to retire in the next few years. His ongoing avoidance to maintain good health and well being was often highlighted to him by his family members. Who each had encouraged him to slow down or even reduce his hours at work on the odd occasion. The dad did not wish take on board their advice, remaining to carry on with which he thought was the best plan.

Sadly, the dad passed away in the next few days leaving the family devastated, especially Joe's Mum. Both Joe and his siblings took it in turns to stay with their mum to support her with the loss.

A few months on, Joe and one of his brothers spent some time with their mum, supporting her in making plans for the future. It became very clear she had no input to the family finances or savings, as the dad had always taken care of this. As they began to unpick the family finances, what they thought they were going to discover was not the case, as shown briefly below:

Mortgage on the family home had five years and a few months payment outstanding

Three different credit cards with outstanding balances on:

- Holidays
- Clothing
- Home expenses
- Gifts

Bank Loans:

- Children's education
- Family cars

- Three children's costs of living while at university

- Family conservatory

- Savings: £25,500

- Retirement: £45,000

The family were devastated to discover that they were running on a loss. Once the funeral costs and outstanding bills were taken away from any savings, they would still be left with massive debts to be paid out.

Joe just could not get his head around HOW was this possible, so he went to visit one of his dad's friends whom he had worked alongside for many years. He quite simply pointed out that Joe's dad had not planned for the long term. The friend told Joe, "Your dad had a very good salary, but did not educate himself about growing his finances. If he had taken this opportunity on board, things for your father and family could have looked very different. "What do you mean?" Joe asked.

He went on to share some examples of what the dad could have done to make his financial future more secure:

- Life insurance

- Work bonus schemes

- Investing in company shares

- Letting your mum work and create her own financial security

- Letting you and your siblings earn money before you all arrived in your late twenties

- Savings

- Reducing expenses and life luxuries instead of increasing them year on year

"Don't get me wrong Joe, your dad was a very respected man and built a great reputation across hundreds of clients at the firm, but every hour he had was tied up doing something for someone else, and he always wanted to give everyone one of you the best, so instant spending became his rescue plan, but this turned into a lifelong habit.

Reflection Exercise Two

Give some other examples of how Joe Flash can move forward from this so he does not repeat the same pattern as his dad?

1.

2.

3.

"What we really want to do is what we are really meant to do. When we do what we are meant to do, money comes to us, doors open for us, we feel useful and the work we do feels like play to us"

- Julia Cameron

The Average Family

Let's look at a family who compound financial education into their everyday lives on a daily basis, while discovering ways to chase their dreams. Meet the Average family and their only son, Alvin.

Strong willed, confident and quick to learn, Alvin loved to discover and was always asking lots of questions. He was a child who made an impact wherever he went.

School reports would display Alvin's eagerness to learn, achieve and participate within his school environment. He was also a popular child who had many friends. Teachers would often tell Alvin's mum that he was a well rounded young boy.

At home with his family, he loved to ask lots of questions about what they were doing and why. He enjoyed being surrounded by his close and extended family members. They all had such a variety of talents, hobbies, occupations and businesses, which gave Alvin a panoramic view of different ways of living.

Aged seven, Alvin started his first paid job: emptying the family bins. He was very happy as the first few months went by, but when the cold winter came along he was tempted to give it up as it was much warmer inside than up the drive with the bins!

Aged eight, he had an idea about how to make some more money. Sharing his thoughts with his family, he began write a plan. Little did Alvin know that he was about to make his first investment by taking the profits he had earned from the bin job to buy what he needed to make his idea work. Once Alvin had written down everything he needed, he took a trip to the local shops with his mum to purchase ingredients and nice packaging. His idea was to make and sell cakes on Halloween using a secret recipe once given to him by a family member.

Halloween morning arrived, and Alvin was busy baking with his mum in the kitchen. His plan was to have all the cakes ready to start selling in the local area by early evening. Alvin loved to bake and was feeling very excited about the day ahead. With a family member on hand, he was all packed up and ready to sell his cakes just after his tea.

Taking the lead, he started going from door to door to sell, with family watching him in the background. He was greeted with many refusals and doors that just stayed shut. Alvin soon realised it was not going as easily as he had hoped. Undeterred, he carried on. Arriving at a new street, things began to improve. His cake sales began to pick up, and some people were even buying double packs. This lifted Alvin's spirits so he carried on. As the evening started to draw in, he had a few cakes left so he reduced the prices for the last few houses. He felt great, as he had doubled his profits way over what he was hoping for, and also had a bag full of other treats that had been given to him along the way.

Alvin shared his cake sales success story with his family at a get-together. His uncle Steve, who had his own business, saw great potential in Alvin so he spent some time teaching him about financial principles. Laying out Alvin's piggy banks that had been given to him on different birthdays over the years, Uncle Steve labeled each piggy bank with a different name.

- Giving
- Investing
- Saving
- Spending

Like most children, Alvin was enjoying the moment spending time and learning new things with his uncle, while being a little bit fascinated that his piggy banks had just had a makeover. Unknown to Alvin, he was learning his first very valuable wealth principle.

Uncle Steve said, "Alvin, every time you earn or receive money, I want you to put 10% of it into each of your piggy banks. "Why?" Alvin asked. Steve replied, "To have more of the things you love, you must be able to make good choices with what you already have."

Alvin was not fully sure what this meant, but the word MORE sounded good to him, so he made a start, sticking to this over the rest of his childhood.

Here's what he used it for:

- Giving

By sponsoring two children from Rwanda with the youth group he was part of, he was giving his 10%

- Investing

Making and selling homemade lemonade, cookies, and cakes

- Saving

For holidays and computer games

- Spending

Sweets, toys and days out

"It's not how much money you make but how much money you keep. How hard it works for you and how many generations you keep it for."

- Robert Kiyosaki

Alvin was encouraged to dream big, believe in himself and pursue all the things he loved. He also enjoyed playing football with his friends, visiting adventure trails and cooking. Alvin would often dream that when he was older, he would own a restaurant with a hotel attached.

Aged sixteen, he started at college to train as a chef and study business. A few months into college, he started working a weekend job in the city at a small restaurant to gain new experience and knowledge towards starting his own restaurant. Every few months, Alvin would leave his job to move to a higher paid chef's role in different restaurants. Keeping his living cost very low was something he had been shown when he was little. His social time would consist of meeting up with friends, playing football or just relaxing at home reading or cooking. Though the days of using a piggy bank were now over, he was still using the same financial principles from when he was eight. Alvin was now redirecting his income into his high interest bank accounts.

1.   **Spending account**
        Giving + 10%
        Investing + 10%
        Food
        Rent
        Clothing
        Travel
        Phone
2.   **Holiday saving account + 10%**
3.   **Business saving account + 10%**
4.   **Networth account + 10%**

Any money Alvin would receive through jobs or a return on investments, he'd take out 10% of the total figure firstly to give back, then also put 10% back into his investments and lastly would transfer 10% to each of his other accounts, holiday savings, business savings and his networth.

In the back of his wallet, Alvin carried the value for a three night stay at his hotel and for a three course meal at his restaurant. He did this to make a personal statement of integrity and belief in the value of his vision and the services they would one day offer customers.

> *"If money management isn't something you enjoy, consider my perspective. The time you spend monitoring your finances will pay off. You can make real money by cutting expenses and earning more interest on savings and investments. I'd challenge you to find a part time job where you could potentially earn as much money for just an hour or two of your time"*

> **- Laura D. Adams**

Once Alvin finished at college, he decided to take a year out to travel and to explore different cultures, experience new tastes and learn from different people around the globe. Using his holiday savings, he set off on his travels. In fourteen months, he had visited many new cities. He took on paid work in cafes or restaurants to satisfy his eagerness to learn, gathering ideas to use towards the opening of his own restaurant. A few weeks after returning home from traveling, Alvin decided that now was the time to get started, so he wrote out his business plan for the restaurant and hotel, setting a goal to open in the year of his twenty first birthday.

Getting Started:

Financing the business, Alvin used:

- Business savings

- Return from his stocks and shares

- Child investment shares which his parent had placed 10% every month into his child funds account for twenty years

- Gift from his parent who had saved 10% into a high interest savings account every month for twenty years

- Alvin also had accepted an offer from an investor named Frankie

Meeting Frankie - Investor

Alvin had meet Frankie a few years ago when working weekends in a restaurant. One day, Alvin's head chef pointed out one of the customers to him who happened to be a big business player who owned several restaurants. Alvin was intrigued, so boldly went over to speak to him, leaving his head chef a bit surprised. Alvin walked over to introduce himself. Reaching out to shake his hand, he introduced himself, briefly explaining his restaurant dream, and asked him about how he got started in business.

Frankie, a very busy man and not normally the social type, was quite blown away that Alvin came over to talk to him. When their conversion began, Frankie took a shine to Alvin, answered some of his questions and gave him his business card. During Alvin's time at college and traveling, he sent the odd short email to Frankie, to let him know what he was doing and where he was up to in his business plans. Once Alvin had finished his business plans, he called Frankie to arrange a meeting. That call was the start of a great partnership and friendship. Alvin still had a lot to learn, but Frankie believed in him and his vision and knew he had a lot of potential, so was prepared to take the risk to invest in and mentor Alvin to achieve this dream.

Eight Years On...

Alvin's restaurant and hotel was open and thriving with four other sites which had taken off across the UK. It was a joy for visitors, holiday makers, business delegates and families to stay there. Alvin was now married with two beautiful children, a self-made millionaire. They had a beautiful family home just outside of the city with great views, not too big not and not too small with the mortgage already paid off. The family car was pre-owned and bought outright from a reputable car dealer. Any time the family wanted to change the car, Alvin would challenge this dealer to search for the best car at the lowest price.

They enjoyed keeping their leisure activities fairly basic; walking the dogs, field sports or running. A family who was not excessively concerned about material possessions or excessive spending, defining their life by keeping their living expenses low and their giving and savings high.

As a family, they enjoyed days out going for walks and picnics, weekends camping, visiting friends or hosting social time for family and friends at their home. Alvin encouraged and supported his wife to own her independence outside of being with him or the children, by pursing her own enjoyments, hobbies, social time, investments and career choice. His wife also ran a business alongside her close friend. It was a little boutique in their local area where she spent her time while the children were at school or with their dad.

Average Family Financial Guide: Spending account:

A spending account is a great way to:

1. Keep track of your spending habits outside of your everyday living expenses.
2. Practice giving to those in need.
3. Review each month how much money you can save by keeping your expenses minimal.

Savings account - 10% from all earnings transferred

A savings account is a great way to create financial security for yourself:

First, transfer a minimum of two months outgoings into your account. If anything ever comes up, you know you're covered for two months. (e.g. redundancy, sickness, career change)

Once you have achieved the first step, then add more savings for something you want to treat yourself with, such as holidays and hobbies.

Business savings account - 10% from all earnings transferred:

Set up your business cash flow to match your long term plans/goals:

- Outline what you're saving for, why and how much
- Become investment ready

Networth account - 10% From All Earnings Transferred:

A networth account is a great way to see:

- Your personal value of living
- Whether your personal value is increasing through gaining experience

As your skills and knowledge increase, so will your earnings! Many people, self employed or business owners, make the mistake of thinking that when their earnings increase, they can spend more. This is a potentially dangerous way of thinking. Though spending can be fun in the here and now, it is a drain on your finances in the long term. When you are playing to win, it pays off for your future to review your value every three to six months. It would help to stop and ask yourself these three questions regarding your finances:

1. Am I adding more value to others?

2. Are my abilities strengthening, developing and increasing?

3. Is my income increasing?

Give yourself a pay rise by increasing your transferring percentages from 10% to 15%. By compounding these personal pay raises yearly or three or five years "you choose", give yourself the future scope to live each day on only 5% of your left over income. Having 95% of your income streams left over to give more, save more and increase your personal networth.

If you're new to understanding how to make your money work for you, maybe start off by transferring 2% or 5% across your accounts as your starting point. Set a reminder date or a note to yourself when you're due to receive your next personal pay rise. DON'T wait for someone else to tell you what you're worth. You may be waiting a long time! Start building your own wealth as you build your successful business. As you do so, associate yourself with those who are financially educated, and continue to study the art of living financially free.

*"Wealth consists not in having great
possessions, but having fewer wants"*

- Epictetus

Budgeting is the starting point, and the foundation from which to begin growing your wealth, and yet many people don't think to find ways for their money to work for them in the long term. Sometimes this can be seen as more hard work, much like having to take the washing out or walk the dog. The idea of budgeting can initially cause one to envision having to give things up, and deny oneself enjoyment, this is not the case at all! Budgeting actually puts you in control because it allows you to choose how and where you allocate your money. Making choices about how to use your finances will save you the grief that can be the result of overspending and attracting debt.

The world has hundreds, millions and billions of pounds available for anyone of us. The only person holding you back from receiving is you. There is no better time to change your financial future than to now.

Educate, Commit, Repeat, Repeat...

Anita Frost

Reflection Exercise Three:

Here is an example of what an average budget plan can look like.

Budget Plan	Jan	Feb	Mar	Apr	May
Food					
Phone					
Gas					
Electric					
TV					
Food Expenses					
Wellbeing/Fitness					
Clothing					
Petrol					
Car					
Tax					
Insurance					
Holidays					
Total					
Investments					
Property					
Business					
Training					
Books					
Total					

Jun	July	Aug	Sept	Oct	Nov	Dec

Anita Frost

Budget Plan	Jan	Feb	Mar	Apr	May
Networth					
Back Of Your Wallet					
Savings					
Personal					
Child					
Business					
Giving					
Church/Tithing					
Charity					
Total					
Investments - Returns					
Property					
Business					
Books					
Total					

Jun	July	Aug	Sept	Oct	Nov	Dec

CHAPTER FIVE

THE ROAD LESS TRAVELED

Do the difficult things while they are easy and do the great things when they are small. A journey of a thousand miles must begin with a single step

- Lao Tzu

This is your time to step out onto the road less traveled. An entrepreneur's journey has no final destination - each experience they encounter can change their course of direction at any time, opening new doors to lead them into new places. The change of direction inspires them to seek and discover more than they set out to find. Entrepreneurs never aim to complete their ideas, but find ways to expand them through innovation and risk-taking as much as they can.

The time for adventure is now! As excitement fuels you, will you travel with your hands gripped to the stirring wheel, nose nearly touching the window, or will you let the roof down to feel the wind on your face and maybe drop into cruise control to go with the flow? Entrepreneurs often have both hands gripped tight when bends and turns approach them at speed, but letting the roof down and enjoying the wind in their hair after each challenge passes them. Long journeys are not always the comfiest, and we are often advised to take lots of short breaks in between in order to break up the journey, allow ourselves to stay refreshed, and prevent our bodies seizing up.

As an entrepreneur, you will experience times of discomfort, so schedule regular breaks to refuel and refresh your thinking before the next move is to be made. Successful business people see and understand the benefits of taking part in regular exercise to de-stress and maximise peak performance. Understanding and knowing how to get the best out of themselves, they must consistently serve their bodies well in order to be in the best condition to continue their journey.

Remember in Chapter Three when we read the story of the caterpillar who masters the art of allowing to complete their journey to become a butterfly?

Maybe you have:

- Just started your business venture
- Been building your venture for some time
- Completely given up on your dreams

Lots of entrepreneurs climb mountains to reach their dreams, but reach the top of the mountain only to realize they were on the wrong mountain in the first place. At this point, many give up or become disheartened and are tempted to give up climbing. The guidance within this book is designed to set you on your course to climb again. You are now collecting enough knowledge and understanding to realign you in stepping out on to the right mountain. *Your mountain.*

Savannah's Journey

The right road for one is the wrong road for another...the journey of life is not paved in blacktop; it is not brightly lit, and it has no road signs. It is a rocky path through the wilderness.

M. Scott Peck

I sat on the edge of my bed and tried my best to settle the butterflies that were swirling around my stomach. "Savannah!", my dad shouted from below, "Get a move on. the taxi is waiting". I stood up and looked out of the window. He was right - there it was. The driver, revving the engine, looked annoyed that he was kept waiting. Rolling my eyes, I shouted back, "alright I'm coming!"

"What were you doing up there?" laughing nervously, he looked puzzled.

"I was thinking that maybe it's not such a good idea after all"

He put his arm around me and gave me a squeeze. "What are you talking about? Of course you are going! You're all packed." I looked down at the bags around me. The taxi beeping outside disturbed my thoughts.

"Yes, I was thinking it would be as easy to put everything back as it was packing"

My dad smiled, and his eyes began to fill up. "Savannah, as much as I don't want you to go, I've got to let you. You're all grown up now and it's your time, your moment to go and get your dream."

I smiled, "but, what if I don't want my dream anymore?... what if..."

My dad stopped me. "There are no 'if's! You wouldn't have packed in the first place if there were! Now go on", he said picking up my bags and escorting me out of the door.

"What? You're kicking me out!" I laughed. "Anyone would think you wanted to get rid..."

He stopped me mid-sentence. "No, no, I just don't want you to regret not going. I'll be here when you get back. This house will be here when you get back...I'll see you soon."

He gave me the biggest hug I can recall, and I almost didn't want to let go until the taxi beeped for its final time.

"Come on, lady!" the taxi man shouted, "I could have done double the jobs by now."

I turned back to my dad. "Ok". I smiled, putting on a brave face. "Here I go!", I shouted, trying to hold back my tears. I gave him one last hug and quickly walked to the taxi.

I was excited. I couldn't wait to get to America, the land of dreams, but at the same time I was terrified. I was going to be alone for the first time in eighteen years. I waved as the taxi pulled away and watched as my dad and the town I grew up in disappeared into the background.

> *Almost everything worthwhile carries with it some sort of risk, whether it's starting a new business, whether it's leaving home, whether it's getting married, or whether it's flying in space.*

> **- Chris Hadfield**

It was quiet in the taxi, and I got lost in my thoughts thinking about the opportunities I would come face to face with. Applying for the position to become a fashion designer in America last year, I believed it was my time. I knew this position was made for me. A few months passed after applying, and I heard nothing which made me become slightly downhearted, but I knew I was meant to travel and share my ideas for fashion. A few months later I received a letter. Completely shocked but so excited, I had been chosen. They obviously had seen potential.

I couldn't wait to go and get out of the town I had grown up in. I could not help but tell everyone and anyone about what I was about to do. Although thinking back now, friends that I thought were friends did become distant and didn't seem to share the same excitement about my opportunity. I didn't let it bother me too much, or at least I didn't even think about it until now.

"So where are you off to, love?"

My thoughts disturbed, I looked up and the taxi driver was looking through the rear-view mirror and grinning like the Cheshire cat out of Alice in Wonderland. That made me laugh, and although he looked a little crazy, he put me at ease.

"New York, America" I said.

"You don't look like you are sure" he laughed. "Do you want me to turn around?" I didn't say a thing. My eyes widened and I just smiled. No way was I turning back! Well not today, anyway.

"I'm good, you can keep going".

He took his eyes from the mirror.

"That is a great answer", he said. "So what is taking you to America?"

I really didn't feel like talking but felt rude not answering, so I explained my situation about leaving my dad, my friends' reactions, and some of my fears and doubts. He listened to me without interrupting and added his own thoughts about not listening to anyone else, trusting my own instincts, and carrying on no matter what to follow through with my dreams.

"You shouldn't care what your friends think. If they can't support you, then they were not meant to be a part of the next chapter of your journey".

I thought, "okay so now maybe I like this taxi man. He speaks sense".

"Your home is where your heart is, but your future is on the plane".

Feeling confident and happy as we pulled up outside the airport, my palms began to sweat as I found my purse to pay, cheekily smiling to myself and thinking, "this is it, Savannah!!!"

> *Transformation is a process, and as life happens there are tons of ups and downs. It's a journey of discovery – there are moments on mountain tops and moments in deep valleys of despair.*

- Rick Warren

The taxi driver placed my cases to the side. I reach out to hand him his fare.

Smiling, he said, "you be safe and have a great time."

"Thank you", I said.

As I collected my bags, the airport doors opened. The place was manic with the fuss and rush of people getting to the right places. There were crowds everywhere and I figured that if I was actually going to get to my plane, I'd better get a move on...

Many hours later, Savannah arrives in America...

....Feeling a little dizzy and even a bit sick to my stomach as I watched people rush around the airport, I must have looked like a lost puppy as everyone else seemed to know where they were going. I took a deep breath and made my way over to the exit. As the doors automatically opened, I was blinded by the sun's rays and hit by the heat. I was finally here in the land of my opportunity!

My goal, for a long time, had been to break into the design industry. Smiling, I already knew I had made it - I just had to make it official, and with that I hailed a taxi. I asked the driver to take me to the College of Fashion, Art and Design. This was one of the leading colleges in America. My stomach began to turn again. I couldn't wait to get there and unpack, explore, and meet new people.

Plan Ahead

Walking around the college filled me with inspiration. I had such a wonderful feeling of being at home - it felt like somewhere I automatically belonged. The walls were filled with stunning world class designs on display. I began to visualize my design being on display with my name "Savannah Armond" written on a gold shine plaque next to my design.

Once I had collected my timetable, local maps and other bits of information, I visited the cafe to sit down and study the information and familiarise myself with the maps, planning all the routes I would be taking around the college. I was so looking forward to getting properly started on the course. I was not due to start officially for three weeks, so I was looking forward to spending that time exploring the city and getting settled in.

Embrace Change

When I got back to my room, I pulled the curtain back. There was an incredible and breathtaking view of the New York streets, so busy and alive. When I opened my case, I started to cut out some of my favourite designs from the Vogue magazine I had read earlier on the plane. Pulling out some paper from my notepad, I wrote *I am a Fashion Designer, I create world class designs*, and *people love to buy my collections* and stuck them around my new workspace.

First term started, and I felt like a sponge absorbing so much new information. Our first assignment was to prepare a presentation to feed back to the rest of the class. Preparing for my presentation seemed like the worst week of my life. The thoughts of standing up in front of everyone made me feel sick. All kinds of worrying thoughts filled my head. What would happen if I forgot what I was going to talk about? What if everyone started laughing at me?

As I sat at my desk in my room later on, I looked back at the notes I had written when I first arrived. *I am a Fashion Designer. I create world class designs. People love to buy my collections.* I started to say them out loud, wondering if the people next door would think I was crazy if they heard me. Anyway, it gave me a good feeling and besides, anything was better than listening to my brain trying to freeze me up.

When presentation day came, I enjoyed listening to other students in the class as they shared their presentations before it was my turn. My palms started to clam up and my face felt like I had just entered a sauna and those fearful thoughts flooded back. All I wanted was to walk out and run back to my room. My tutor must have seen my agony, because she told the class to take a quick ten minutes break, and then walked over to me and encouraged me to believe in myself and to share my passion in the way only I knew how. "When you do, the others will believe in you too", she said.

My presentation went so well, the class all clapped, That day, I had learnt so much about myself through the challenge. I could not wait to get to the phone and tell my family what I had achieved, and how grateful I was to my tutor who had helped me to have the courage to go ahead with it at the last minute.

Appreciate the bumps in the road

The first term of college had flown by as I was learning such a lot from my new experiences, especially at work. When I started, I was a little disheartened with the role I had been assigned. In hindsight, I can see that fetching coffee and running mundane errands was actually a great opportunity to learn from observation how the industry works in practice. Walking in and out of the offices of some of the top designers was so inspiring. I would think to myself that I could be in one of those offices one day if I do my best with what I have been given to do now. There were a few times I wanted to give up, but encouragement came from my new college friends and family back home. I stuck to my plan and added more pictures and statements to the brick alcove of my work space. These included pictures of what I saw my first office looking like, as well as runway events and a shop window with one of my designs on display.

As each college year passed, my outlook, vision and self belief grew massively...

Follow the Signposts

One of the fashion designers at work had been given the opportunity to start designing for a famous fashion house in Italy, and would be leaving at the end of the month. The management team opened the vacancy to the fashion students first. I could hardly contain myself as I took an application pack, That evening when I returned back to my room and opened the application pack, I saw that the requirement was to submit six collection items as if preparing them for a runway event.

I was due to finish college in the next two months, so the vacancy had come at just the right time. If I wanted to stay in New York and achieve my goals, this was my chance. I had college work, lectures and my part-time job, so I had to use any free time I could get to work on the collection, Feeling exhausted, I put my all in financially, emotionally and physically to submit my work for the vacancy, With four days left till the closing date, I had two whole collections to finish. I called home close to tears, ready to melt down. My dad gave me some encouragement, saying "you can only do your best, Savannah".

> *"If you're working on something exciting that you really care about, you don't have to be pushed; the vision pulls you"*
> **- Steve Jobs**

After talking with my dad, I went to the cafe to have some time out and clear my thoughts. I looked into my drink, thinking over all I had achieved since arriving in New York, becoming deeply grateful for everything and everyone who had been apart of my journey. After finishing my drink, I started to walk back to my room and noticed that a new collection display had gone up on the other side of the cafe.

For some reason it pulled me to go over. As I drew closer and realised it was the collection we had done last term as part of our studies. I looked up and saw my name, "Savannah Armond" with my design framed next to it. This was such an honor, because with over fifty students in our group, only twelve designs had been selected for display and one of them was mine! After seeing this, I could not wait to get back and finish the collection ready for the closing date in a few days.

Stay on course

Two weeks went by, and I heard nothing back about my application, One afternoon while in the kitchen making some drinks at work, the lady from reception said that the chief executive from the events team wanted to see me. "What for?" I asked, a little confused, as no one goes to see this person because he is in a different department to the design team. When I reached his office, his PA greeted me and said I could go in. Opening the door, I saw two other people; one who I had not seen before, and the head designer. The head designer said, "Hello Savannah thank you for coming to see us. We wanted to let you know we are delighted with your application, and we are very pleased to offer you a role as fashion designer here at the store. We also want to use your collection at the next runway event in six weeks time". I accepted the offer, trying to contain my excitement as they talked me through what would happen next. From that moment, everything completely changed for me.

The week before the runway event, my family flew over to see me and stay for the event, which was a huge success. My collection was scouted by top retailers. This promotion and the pay that came with it allowed me to move into a two-floored apartment, which was the exact same apartment that I had cut out from a magazine three years ago and stuck on the wall of my work space when I started college. One floor was for living, and the other was for my work.

To think how far I'd come forward from being in a new country and a new college by myself. Here I was now living my dream for real! I owe a lot to the wonderful friends and mentors who encouraged me to stay focused and persistent along the way.

"Patience, persistence and perspiration make
an unbeatable combination for success"
Napoleon Hill

CHAPTER SIX

Visualise and Set Goals

Start with something small and basic such as an apple. Look at the apple from different angles and points, and once you have a clear image, bring your focus closer towards the apple, looking at its skin. Is it smooth or rough? Are there any holes? Is it a green apple or a red one? **Focus on details**. This works to engage your creativity while exercising your visualisation skills. **Spend time** observing the details. That way, you will learn to stay **focused** on the visualisation exercise and not let irrelevant thoughts distract you.

When you begin to have very few distractions at all during your times of visualisation, you have made great progress. If this is your first time working on these skills and you realise that you cannot focus for long, or hold the images you want, this is a sign that you just need more practise exercising these skills.

Tips

- Draw out what you see before trying the hold the image in your mind
- Play music to support your senses
- Find a place you feel most relaxed
- Explore ways to spark your creativity

The Power of Visualising

There is a recurring theme around gaining excellent performance across many professions. Several top achievers know the importance of picturing themselves already playing the part, using their visualisation to accelerate the vision towards reality. Applying belief, creativity and imagination, they repetitively play the image over.

"You have got to be hungry for ideas, to make things happen to your vision made into a reality"

- Anita Roddick

Anita Roddick started The Body Shop in 1976 simply to create a livelihood for herself and her two daughters, while her husband Gordon was trekking across the Americas. She had no training or experience and her only business acumen was Gordon's advice to take sales of £300 a week. Nobody then talked of entrepreneurship as survival, but that's exactly what it is and what nurtures creative thinking. Running that first shop taught her that business is about creating a product or service so good that people will pay for it. Over 30 years later, The Body Shop became a multi local business with over 2.045 stores serving over 77 million customers in 51 different countries in 25 different languages and across 12 time zones.

Her success came from more than just a good idea. Planning and timing were key too. The Body Shop arrived just as Europe was becoming increasingly aware of environmental issues. The Body Shop has always been recognisable by its green colour, the only colour that they could find to cover the damp, mouldy walls of her first shop. Anita opened a second shop within six months, by which time her husband Gordon was back in England. He came up with the idea for 'self-financing' more new stores, which sparked the growth of the franchise network through which The Body Shop spread across the world. The company went public in 1984. Anita Roddick, as well as being a visionary entrepreneur, was an activist and a storyteller. Her legacy is a wonderful example of what one small business owner can accomplish when transferring experiences to create ideas, applying innovation and dedication to her team and the products and services her customers received.

"Whatever you do be different, if you're different you will stand out"

- Anita Roddick

Put On Your Future Shoes:

As children get into the moment of play, becoming a superhero, a shopkeeper, or a favorite animal, they love nothing more than to welcome friends and family or add others toys into the game to bring more life and fun. Allowing their imaginations to run free, they follow each thought, using blankets to make dens, cushions to become cars, and toy boxes to be rocketships.

The left hand side of the brain is used to hold and form words, logic, numbers, sequence, analysis, and lists. Growing up, we significantly increase the use of our left hand side of the brain and use the **creative** and **imaginative** right side of our brains less and less. We persuade ourselves that it is silly or uncomfortable to role play, so much so, that if, for example, the word **role play** comes up in team building exercises or at an interview, we would become embarrassed and freeze up.

In the Disney animation of Cinderella, she spends years serving her ugly sisters. Through every request and demand they put on to her she smiles, sings and carries on serving them. Her relentless positivity, joy and daydreaming sets her up for a night she could only dream about. Her fairy godmother gives her the perfect outfit, travel arrangements and all the trimmings for one night at the ball. All Cinderella's visualising and role play with her broom leads her up to having the night of her dreams. As the night draws to a close, Cinderella leaves behind her shoe, not just any shoe "a shoe" designed for purpose, made to fit only her. She is required to put on her future shoes to move into what is awaiting for her next. No matter who else tried to fit into her shoe, the shoe was made to fit the one who did the work carried vision, and kept moving with a positive attitude.

Many get caught up or lost in the fantasy of having lots of money, big houses and top of the range cars, and the desires to accumulate these things pulls them to focus on simply enjoying the idea of spending or receiving things, but no amount of fantasising can make it happen. To bring your vision to pass requires you to keep working smartly and continuing to invest in your personal development.

Manage and Develop Yourself

- Learn the art of effective communication and leadership
- Increase positive thinking and actions
- Hold and grow your finances
- Take the road less travelled
- Visualise and set goals

Richard Branson, a successful entrepreneur who loves risk taking, founded his business empire with a string of creative ideas, imagination, hard work and determination which put him into the history books.

During a conference, Branson shared his story of how Virgin Airlines began:

"I was in my late twenties and I had a business, but nobody knew who I was then. I was heading to the Virgin islands where I had a lovely girl waiting for me, and I was determined to arrive on time. At the airport, the final flight to the Virgin islands had been cancelled due to maintenance issues or something. I thought this was ridiculous, so went and chartered a private plane to take me to the Virgin islands even though I did not have the money to do so. Then, I picked up a small blackboard, wrote 'Virgin airlines $29" on it and went over to the group of people who had been on the flight that was cancelled. Selling tickets to fill the rest of the seats in the plane, I was able to pay the cost of hiring the chartered plane, and we all traveled to the Virgin islands that night."

From 1966 to 2015, Richard Branson has a timeline of fifty-nine attempts in entrepreneurship, and yet he never gave upon his imaginative and creative ideas.

Create A Dream Collage - What do I Want?

This can be put together on a piece of large or small thick paper, card or board. Use describing words that are in line with the person you are, what you stand for, and what you want to become. Then add pictures of places, themes, investments and opportunities you desire to experience.

You can draw these yourself, or you can cut them out from magazines or whatever you can find. Once you are happy with your vision collage, place it somewhere you can see it on a daily basis. This can be added to or expanded on as your journey gets underway.

Visualising your dreams - let all your senses get involved:

1. Touch

2. Sound

3. Sight

4. Smell

5. Taste

Release Emotions:

1. Laugh

2. Smile

3. Celebrate as if the milestone is done

Use affirmations

Using effective affirmations to powerfully clarify and release your own potential can help support you to harmonise your actions with your goals. A great place to start is by writing your affirmations out on paper to overturn any negative or self doubting beliefs you currently have toward yourself, such as "too lazy" or "not good enough to compete with opponents". Write each one into an "I am" statement that describes what you want to have or experience. Aim to affirm the feeling of already having, for example, " I am active". " I am worthy of a great life". To keep it positive, leave words like 'no', 'not', 'never', 'don't', 'won't', and 'can't' out of your vocabulary, as these types of words push what you are aiming for further away from your reach. Write out your affirmations to be what is believable to you, then seek out quotes which inspire you, fixing them in places you often visit such as the office, fridge or mirror. Speak out statements that you wish to see happen, say each one as if you have already achieved your goal.

As you adapt yourself and learn what's required to propel you along with your business pursuit, your outlook will adjust to becoming wiser and more enthusiastic about life. Your values will strengthen as you adjust your declarations to align with your growth.

Examples:

- "I am a positive person unaffected by the negativity of others"
- "I am enjoying being the creator of my own reality"
- "I love what I do, I do what I love"
- "I am worthy of love and respect "
- "I am surrounded by people who inspire and educate me"
- "I am receiving, and prosperity of all kinds is drawn to me"

Reflection Exercise One:

Practice writing out some of your own affirmations below:

Goals

Once you have a clear vision for the direction your business is going in and have clarity as to how you're making a difference or impacting the lives of others, the next step is to develop a plan. Your plan is the blueprint of the steps required to reach where you want to be.

Break It Down

We all have goals we aim to achieve. Breaking your plan down into small chunks removes feelings of being overwhelmed or disheartened. Setting goals can increase your motivation to get started, Motivation sets you up to take action, and consistent daily actions move you into momentum to reach your short term goals, Each achievement will automatically set you up to reach your long term and lifelong goals. Define the areas you're working towards as shown below:

Businesss   *Education*   *Health*   *Family*   *Finance*

Reflection Exercise Two:

Ask yourself

1. Why am I setting these goals?

2. What am I aiming to accomplish?

3. Is it worthwhile?

4. Is now the right time for this?

5. Is it a solution to my needs?

Set Your Goals

Follow the next steps to get you started:

Step One: Select one area at a time, eg business goals,

Step Two: Write down everything you're currently aiming to achieve in your business goals

Step Three: Then plan out how each goal is to be achieved by breaking them down within the required categories: *lifelong, long term, short term, monthly, weekly, daily*

Laying out your goals using these techniques allows you to clearly see what you're required to action on a daily basis to start seeing your dreams coming to life. Read through our provided business goals in each category to give you an idea. Once you're happy that you have completed your first area, (eg business), you can move on to the next one of your choice. Look at the provided example to support you getting started.

Reflection Exercise Four:

Life Long

Business Example: *Build a world class business*

Health Example: *Have a balanced, healthy lifestyle*

Finance Example: *Live financially free*

Write your goals here or in the notes section provided towards the back:

Long Term

Business example: *Develop the skills to become a world class business owner*

Health example: *Eat better, be fit,*

Finance example: *Become financially educated*

Write your goals here or in the notes section provided towards the back:

Short Term

Business example: *Open the business*

Health example: *Educate myself on the best food for my lifestyle*

Finance example: *Commit to learning and implement ways to improve my finances*

Write your goals here or in the notes section provided towards the back:

Monthly

Business example: *Find the location, investment*

Health example: *See a nutritionist and wellbeing expert*

Finance example: *Give, budget, save, invest,*

Write your goals here or in the notes section provided towards the back:

Weekly

Business example: *Every monday for six weeks spend time learning about the products, services, industry*

Health example: *Try new vegetables and take part in regular exercise*

Finance example: *Listen, attend or invest in resources to grow my financial education*

Write your goals here or in the notes section provided towards the back:

Daily

Business example: *Say out loud my affirmation and make time to visualize*

Health example: *Celebrate the progress I am making, saying out loud self appreciation statements*

Finance example: *Read a chapter a day for twelve months*

Write your goals here or in the notes section provided towards the back:

Once you have completed all your areas and selected and set your goals, use the daily goals you have now set and rewrite this list to become your daily to do list

Anita Frost

Daily To Do List

1.

2.

3.

4.

5.

6.

7.

8.

9.

10.

It's recommended to have no more than ten small goals to focus on actioning each day to give you the opportunity to complete each one. If this is your first time setting goals or you have been inconsistent in the past, give yourself two or three goals to start with for thirty days to establish the new habit. Find ways to support yourself in achieving your to do list, scheduling them into your daily routine. Set your alarm or reminders to prompt you when they are meant to be completed. Become accountable to yourself and commit to your goals and promises. The only one who can ever stand in the way is you.

Meet The Author

Anita Frost born in Greater Manchester, England a successful entrepreneur known for her success by illustrating "success comes from managing and developing yourself" her influence and teachings reached out to hundreds of others pursuing their passion and talents to create a improved living.

Professional Background

- Retired Social Worker
- Health & Wellbeing Educator
- Founder - Curricula & Co
- Business Awards Winner
- Training Awards Winner
- Featured On TV & Radio
- Author

For More Information On: Anita Frost – Services

www.anitafrost.com

Anita Frost

Anita Frost

Notes:

Notes:

Notes:

Notes:

Anita Frost

Notes:

Notes:

Anita Frost

Notes:

Notes: